ROBIN PAGE

SEEDS MOVE!

Beach Lane Books
New York   London   Toronto   Sydney   New Delhi

A tiny seed can one day become a flower, a fruit, or even a giant tree. Every seed, big or small, contains the beginnings of a new plant.

But a seed needs sunlight, soil, water, and an uncrowded place to put down roots. To find all these things, a seed must leave home. It must move. . . .

A seed hitchhikes.

Spiky **sticktight** seeds snag in a raccoon's fur and hitch a ride. They may travel a long way before they fall off.

A seed shoots.

A human touch, a passing animal, or a gust of wind—the slightest jostle can send **exploding cucumber** seeds shooting from their pods.

A seed catapults.

When the right time comes, the hanging seedpods of the **touch-me-not** flower burst open, catapulting seeds in all directions.

A seed **drifts.**

A coconut—the huge seed of the **palm** tree—drifts on the ocean. If it is lucky, it will wash ashore and land in a perfect spot to become a new tree.

Attached to a **bloodroot** seed is a tasty tidbit that ants love to eat. The seed tricks the ants into dragging it to their underground nest. There the ants eat the snack, and then bury the remaining seed.

A seed burrows.

A seed rolls.

One kind of **African grass** seed looks and smells just like the droppings of an antelope. Dung beetles eat animal droppings, and these seeds fool the beetles into rolling them back to their underground homes, where the seeds can begin to grow.

A seed sinks.

A **lotus** seed drops from its pod and sinks to the bottom of a pond. There it will nestle into the mud and sprout.

A seed hides.

A western scrub jay collects an **acorn**—the seed of an oak tree—and carries it in its beak to a distant place.

The jay then hides the acorn to eat later, burying it in the ground. But the jay forgets where it put some of its acorns, and those seeds may become new oak trees.

A seed floats.

Monkey-ladder seeds drop from their huge pods, landing in the water below. The seeds float on rivers—even across seas—until they take root on faraway shores.

A seed **squirts.**

The **durian** is one of the orangutan's favorite fruits, but its seeds are bitter. The orangutan eats the fruit, and then squirts out the seeds.

A seed scatters.

The spiny mouse nibbles on the fruit of the **taily weed**. But the seeds of this fruit taste terrible, so the mouse spits them out, scattering them all over.

A seed **falls.**

An unlucky mouse
eats a **wheat** seed,
then gets snatched
up by a hungry hawk.

After, the hawk eats the mouse, it coughs up a pellet that contains the mouse's fur and bones— along with the undigested wheat seed. The pellet falls to the ground, where the seed can sprout.

A seed parachutes.

When a **milkweed** pod splits open, it releases hundreds of seeds. Each tiny seed is attached to silken threads that parachute in the wind, carrying the seed far away.

A seed plunges.

The seedpod of the **red mangrove** plunges into the water. The pod will drift away, then settle to the bottom of the marsh and put down roots.

A seed helicopters.

The seeds of a **yang-na** tree helicopter, spinning as they fall. They often end up some distance from their parent tree.

A seed plops.

Throughout the summer and fall, a hungry brown bear eats **mountain ash berries** and other fruits. As the bear wanders in search of more food, the undigested seeds plop out inside large piles of the bear's poop.

And then a seed grows . . .

We also help seeds move and grow! Farmers and gardeners all over the world plant seeds. You can too—try tucking a **watermelon** seed into the soil. Then water it and see what happens.

and grows . . .

and grows!

BEACH LANE BOOKS
An imprint of Simon & Schuster Children's Publishing Division
1230 Avenue of the Americas, New York, New York 10020
Copyright © 2019 by Robin Page
All rights reserved, including the right of reproduction in whole or in part in any form.
BEACH LANE BOOKS is a trademark of Simon & Schuster, Inc.
For information about special discounts for bulk purchases, please contact Simon & Schuster Special
Sales at 1-866-506-1949 or business@simonandschuster.com.
The Simon & Schuster Speakers Bureau can bring authors to your live event. For more information or to
book an event, contact the Simon & Schuster Speakers Bureau at 1-866-248-3049 or visit our website at
www.simonspeakers.com.
Book design by Robin Page
The text of this book is set in Century Gothic.
The illustrations for this book were rendered in Adobe Photoshop.
Manufactured in China
1022 SCP
6 8 10 9 7
Library of Congress Cataloging-in-Publication Data
Names: Page, Robin, 1957– author.
Title: Seeds move! / Robin Page.
Description: First edition. | New York, New York : Beach Lane Books, 2019. | Includes bibliographical
references and index.
Identifiers: LCCN 2018016837 | ISBN 9781534409156 (hardcover : alk. paper)
| ISBN 9781534409163 (eBook)
Subjects: LCSH: Seeds—Dispersal—Juvenile literature.
Classification: LCC QK929.P34 2019 | DDC 581.4/67—dc23 LC record available at
https://lccn.loc.gov/2018016837

For all the children who plant seeds

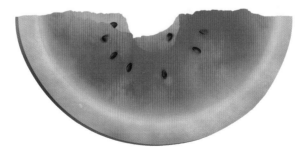